Also by Jane Hirshfield

POETRY

Come, Thief

After

Given Sugar, Given Salt

The Lives of the Heart

The October Palace

Of Gravity & Angels

Alaya

ESSAYS

Ten Windows: How Great Poems Transform the World

Nine Gates: Entering the Mind of Poetry

TRANSLATIONS

The Heart of Haiku (with Mariko Aratani)

Mirabai: Ecstatic Poems (with Robert Bly)

The Ink Dark Moon: Love Poems by Ono no Komachi and Izumi Shikibu, Women of the Ancient Court of Japan (with Mariko Aratani)

ANTHOLOGY

Women in Praise of the Sacred:
43 Centuries of Spiritual Poetry by Women

THE BEAUTY

THE BEAUTY

p o e m s

Jane Hirshfield

Alfred A. Knopf

New York · 2015

THIS IS A BORZOI BOOK
PUBLISHED BY ALFRED A. KNOPF

Copyright © 2015 by Jane Hirshfield
All rights reserved. Published in the United States by Alfred A. Knopf, a division of
Random House LLC, New York, and in Canada by Random House of Canada Limited,
Toronto, Penguin Random House companies.

www.aaknopf.com/poetry

Knopf, Borzoi Books, and the colophon are registered trademarks of Random House LLC.

Library of Congress Cataloging-in-Publication Data
Hirshfield, Jane, 1953–
   [Poems. Selections]
   The beauty : poems / Jane Hirshfield.
      pages cm
   "This is a Borzoi Book"—Title page verso.
   Summary: "A collection of original poems by Jane Hirshfield exploring the profundities
and quirks of existence"—Provided by publisher.
   ISBN 978-0-385-35107-2 (hardback) — ISBN 978-0-385-35108-9 (ebook)
   I. Title.
   PS3558.I694A6 2015
   811'.54—dc23   2014025831

Front-of-jacket image: *Still Life with Peaches* by Adrian Coorte. Private Collection /
Johnny Van Haeften Ltd., London / Bridgeman Images
Author photograph by Michael Lionstar
Jacket design by Stephanie Ross

Manufactured in the United States of America
Published March 18, 2015
Second Printing, April 2015

Contents

———•◆•———

THE BEAUTY

Fado

A man reaches close
and lifts a quarter
from inside a girl's ear,
from her hands takes a dove
she didn't know was there.
Which amazes more,
you may wonder:
the quarter's serrated murmur
against the thumb
or the dove's knuckled silence?
That he found them,
or that she never had,
or that in Portugal,
this same half-stopped moment,
it's almost dawn,
and a woman in a wheelchair
is singing a fado
that puts every life in the room
on one pan of a scale,
itself on the other,
and the copper bowls balance.

My Skeleton

My skeleton,
who once ached
with your own growing larger,

are now,
each year
imperceptibly smaller,
lighter,
absorbed by your own
concentration.

When I danced,
you danced.
When you broke,
I.

And so it was lying down,
walking,
climbing the tiring stairs.
Your jaws. My bread.

Someday you,
what is left of you,
will be flensed of this marriage.

Angular wristbone's arthritis,
cracked harp of rib cage,
blunt of heel,
opened bowl of the skull,
twin platters of pelvis—

each of you will leave me behind,
at last serene.

What did I know of your days,
your nights,
I who held you all my life
inside my hands
and thought they were empty?

You who held me all your life
in your hands
as a new mother holds
her own unblanketed child,
not thinking at all.

My Proteins

They have discovered, they say,
the protein of itch—
natriuretic polypeptide b—
and that it travels its own distinct pathway
inside my spine.
As do pain, pleasure, and heat.

A body it seems is a highway,
a cloverleaf crossing
well built, well traversed.
Some of me going north, some going south.

Ninety percent of my cells, they have discovered,
are not my own person,
they are other beings inside me.

As ninety-six percent of my life is not my life.

Yet I, they say, am they—
my bacteria and yeasts,
my father and mother,
grandparents, lovers,
my drivers talking on cell phones,
my subways and bridges,
my thieves, my police
who chase my self night and day.

My proteins, apparently also me,
fold the shirts.

I find in this crowded metropolis
a quiet corner,

where I build of not-me Lego blocks
a bench,
pigeons, a sandwich
of rye bread, mustard, and cheese.

It is me and is not,
the hunger
that makes the sandwich good.

It is not me then is,
the sandwich—
a mystery neither of us
can fold, unfold, or consume.

Mosquito

I say I
&
a small mosquito drinks from my tongue

but many say we and hear I
say you or he and
hear I

what can we do with this problem

a bowl held in both hands
cannot be filled by its holder

x, says the blue whale
x, say the krill
solve for y, says the ocean, then multiply by existence

the feet of an ant make their own sound on the earth

ice is astonished by water

a person misreads

delirium as delphinium
and falls into
a blueness sleepy as beauty when sneezing

the pronoun dozes

My Eyes

An hour is not a house,
a life is not a house,
you do not go through them as if
they were doors to another.

Yet an hour can have shape and proportion,
four walls, a ceiling.
An hour can be dropped like a glass.

Some want quiet as others want bread.
Some want sleep.

My eyes went
to the window, as a cat or dog left alone does.

MY SPECIES

even
a small purple artichoke
boiled
in its own bittered
and darkening
waters
grows tender,
grows tender and sweet

patience, I think,
my species

keep testing the spiny leaves

the spiny heart

My Corkboard

However many holes are in you,
always there's room for another.

However much you carry,
you can hold more.

Like a saint making a joke,
imperfection of surface
suits you.
Your seams
remind of quiet tectonic plates.

Chthonic corkboard,
always beneath
even when hung on your vertical side,
your waiting thumbtacks
seem to me
a glittering affection,
the *mi casa, su casa*
of a door standing open in every weather
of invitation.

I apologize to you, corkboard—
I, who would like
to be more like you in spirit,
cover you over
with maps, plans, bills.

Even these words that praise you
further disguise you.

My Memory

Like the small soaps and shampoos
a traveler brings home
then won't use,
you, memory,
almost weightless
this morning inside me.

My Weather

Wakeful, sleepy, hungry, anxious,
restless, stunned, relieved.

Does a tree also?
A mountain?

A cup holds
sugar, flour, three large rabbit-breaths of air.

I hold these.

In My Wallet I Carry a Card

In my wallet I carry a card
which declares I have the power to marry.

In my wallet I carry a card
which declares I may drive.

In my wallet I carry a card
that says to a merchant I may be trusted to pay her.

In my wallet I carry a card
that states I can borrow a book in the town where I live.

In my hand I carry a card.
Its lines declare I am cardless, carless,
stateless, and have no money.

It is buoyant and edgeless.
It names me one of the Order of All Who Will Die.

My Task

An idea appears.
It catches
against the edge of the bedside table.

Coffee on the wall.
Coffee on the marble tabletop.
Coffee on the sheets.

The idea has flown everywhere with it.

Aplysia, marine snail of memory,
someone may someday find in your 20,000 neurons
this thought I have lost.

My task to find your less studied sister,
the erasing
and soapy sea sponge.

My Sandwich

So many things
you'd not have thought of
until they were given.

Even the simple—
a cottage cheese sandwich,
a heron's contractible neck.

You eat. You look.
Then you look back and it's over.

This life. This flood—
unbargained for as lasting love was—
of lasting oddness.

A Well Runs Out of Thirst

A well runs out of thirst
the way time runs out of a week,
the way a country runs out of its alphabet
or a tree runs out of its height.
The way a brown pelican
runs out of anchovy-glitter at darkfall.

A strange collusion,
the way a year runs out of its days
but turns into another,
the way a cotton towel's compact
with pot and plate seems to run out of dryness
but in a few minutes finds more.

A person comes into the kitchen
to dry the hands, the face,
to stand on the lip of a question.

Around the face, the hands,
behind the shoulders,
yeasts, mountains, mosses multiply answers.

There are questions that never run out of questions,
answers that don't exhaust answer.

Take this question the person stands asking:
a gate rusting open.
Yes stands on its left, *no* on its right,
two big planets of unpainted silence.

In a Room with Many Windows

In a room with many windows
some thoughts slide past uncatchable, ghostly.
Three silent bicyclists. Slowly, a woman on crutches.
It is like the night you slept out on the sandy edge of a creek bank,
feeling the step of some light, clawed thing on your palm,
crossing to drink. You were nothing to it.
Hummock. Earth clump. Root knob wild in the dark.
Like that thirsty creature, to you.
You could guess it, but you can't name it.

A Photograph of a Face Half Lit, Half in Darkness

Even 3 + 2 is like this.

A photograph of a face half lit, half in darkness.

A train station where one train is stopped
and another passes behind it,
heard, but not seen.

A person proud of five good senses
lives without echolocation.

Dogs pity our noses
as we pity the bee that blunders the glass.

Take out every other word of the world,
what is left?

A half half darkness.

A station one is and passes.

We live our lives in one place
and look in every moment into another.

As on a child's map,
where X
marks both riddle and treasure.

It is near, but not here.

A Cottony Fate

Long ago, someone
told me: avoid *or*.

It troubles the mind
as a held-out piece of meat disturbs a dog.

Now I too am sixty.
There was no other life.

CELLOPHANE: AN ASSAY

There are kinds of transparence.
Yours was invented
sometime between
tempered glass and Saran Wrap.

I have at times wanted to be you:
something looked through and past.

You were born noble: a tree.
Caustics and acids changed you
to what you now are,
protective, stiff, almost weightless.

Both captive and guard,
your desire is to be frivolous, self-destructive,
undone and opened.
Your bright red necklace announces:
"Tear here."

Inside you, tobacco.
Inside you, peppermints, gingersnaps, gum.
You would not be found
wrapping a mattress or gun.

You were dictated into the world
by the muse of "it could be."
You were unlikely but useful,
so kept.

Your art is audible, immodest:
to preserve against time.

In this, you are like a small metal flute
whose throat knows no aging
or a few words
from the second century,
stumbled on once in translation—

"I come from the river, husband,
its brushy bank left these scratches."

Made to be seen through, for pleasure.

QUARTZ CLOCK

The ideas of a physicist
can be turned into useful objects:
a rocket, a quartz clock,
a microwave oven for cooking.
The ideas of poets turn into only themselves,
as the hands of the clock do,
or the face of a person.
It changes, but only more into the person.

My Life Was the Size of My Life

My life was the size of my life.
Its rooms were room-sized,
its soul was the size of a soul.
In its background, mitochondria hummed,
above it sun, clouds, snow,
the transit of stars and planets.
It rode elevators, bullet trains,
various airplanes, a donkey.
It wore socks, shirts, its own ears and nose.
It ate, it slept, it opened
and closed its hands, its windows.
Others, I know, had lives larger.
Others, I know, had lives shorter.
The depth of lives, too, is different.
There were times my life and I made jokes together.
There were times we made bread.
Once, I grew moody and distant.
I told my life I would like some time,
I would like to try seeing others.
In a week, my empty suitcase and I returned.
I was hungry, then, and my life,
my life, too, was hungry, we could not keep
our hands off   our clothes on
our tongues from

Perspective: An Assay

Makes one wall darker than the other,
leaving a corner.
Makes one leaf more red than another, leaving a tree.

Blocks with an earthquake, an illness, a phone call,
what once seemed important.

Holds one perfume close, indelible, while others fade.

Is cubic from every direction, except when rounded.
Sneezes at ardor, boredom, despair.

Cannot in general be found, yet is everywhere local.

Likes magic, for which it is frequently useful.
Likes dice.

Likes everything just as it is, then just as it is, then just as it is.

Enjoys folding anything—
card hands, laundry, letters, elbows and knees.

Hums softly in Giotto, loudly in Tintoretto.
Likes mirrors, windows, old portraits, taking the long view—

This Chinese scroll, for instance, unrolling as if without limit
its small boat, downrushing river, and strolling deep-sleeved officials
in oddly shaped caps,
the curious horse looking out
from behind the long-needled pine it's been momentarily tied to forever.

Ordinary Rain. Every Leaf Is Wet.

The landscape by Dürer
of a dandelion amid grasses

its flowers

done with the first opening
not yet gone into the second

these too will finally bend toward the earth

exiles
writing letters
sent over the mountains by friendly horses and donkeys

Things Keep Sorting Themselves

Does the butterfat know it is butterfat,
milk know it's milk?
No.
Something just goes and something remains.

Like a boardinghouse table:
men on one side, women on the other.
Nobody planned it.

Plaid shirts next to one another,
talking in accents from the Midwest.

Nobody plans to be a ghost.

Later on, the young people sit in the kitchen.

Soon enough, they'll be the ones
to stumble *Excuse me* and quickly withdraw.
But they don't know that.
No one can ever know that.

I Wake Early

I wake early,
make two cups of coffee,
drink one,
think, go back to sleep,
wake again, think,
drink the other.

To start a day over
is a card game played for no money,
a ripe tomato,
a swimming cat.

Time here:
lukewarm,
with milk and sugar,
big and unset as a table.

I wake twice.

Twice the window
unbroken, transparent.

Twice the cat's nose and ears above water.
Twice the war (my war)
is distant,
its children's children are distant.

In a Kitchen Where Mushrooms Were Washed

In a kitchen where mushrooms were washed,
the mushroom scent lingers.

As the sea must keep for a long time the scent of the whale.

As a person who's once loved completely,
a country once conquered,
does not release that stunned knowledge.

They must want to be found, those strange-shaped, rising morels,
clownish puffballs.

Lichens have served as a lamp-wick.
Clean-burning coconuts, olives.
Dried salmon, sheep fat, a carcass of petrel set blazing:
light that is fume and abradement.

Unburnable mushrooms are other.
They darken the air they come into.

Theirs the scent of having been traveled, been taken.

HONEY

Music comes with instructions:
pianissimo, forte.

In Nō plays the actors wear masks,
so their souls can be seen:
wild-haired old woman, callow young priest.

Each morning I wake in strange country,
my bed made of strange wood.
Time arrives clockless.
Rain poses hieroglyphic, with bent knees,
shoulders askew, arms lifting
from out of the future
the future—

a box labeled neither
"Requests" nor "Suggestions."

What is, what will be,
is honey.
Touched, it sticks to the fingers.

Andromeda overhead, silent.
Below, ears, eyes,
an aching elbow,
Chekhov, the laboring bees.

HAMPER

As sunlight or darkness fits itself
around lamp, table, or mountain,

silence stitches itself
around hopes, thoughts, and words.

Some hear it
the sound of their own speech
coming back from where they are dead.

Some find it summer-cool pillow,
winter wool coat.

Some tack their names
on its door and step inside.

And if in that room there is happiness
so without measure
you cannot keep your eyes open to see it,

and if in that room sorrow bends
like late nettles in sleet,

the silence will be there also to greet them,

setting each in its wicker hamper
on a plaid blanket, two sleepy puppies.

Florists' Roses

color of a library wall
in Venice

bred
to stay on the stem

hands of an old woman
on an old chicken
pull them off

"for the petals"
she says

while remembering
the sudden mercilessness
between lovers

Mop Without Stick

I am on my knees again,
mop without stick,
over old fir trees turned into flooring.
A thought stood once in the middle,
near the cookstove, left heel and right heel.
Left hand and right hand, I wash around it.
Thought without handle,
thought without hands, without lemons or Serengeti.
One breath, another,
one corner of cotton in water wets the whole cloth.

THE PROBLEM

You are trying to solve a problem.
You're almost certainly halfway done,
maybe more.

You take some salt, some alum,
and put it into the problem.
Its color goes from yellow to royal blue.

You tie a knot of royal blue into the problem,
as into a Peruvian quipu of colored string.

You enter the problem's bodegas,
its flea markets, souks.
Amid the alleys of sponges and sweets,
of jewelry, spices, and hair combs,
you ponder which stall, which pumpkin or perfume, is yours.

You go inside the problem's piano.
You choose three keys.
One surely must open the door of the problem,
if only you knew only this:
is the quandary edible or medical,
a problem of reason or grief?

It is looking back at you now
with the quizzical eyes of a young, bright dog.

Her whole body pitched for the fetch,
the dog wants to please.
If only she could ascertain which direction,

what object, which scent of riddle,
and if the problem is round or elliptical in its orbit,
and if it is measured in foot-pounds, memory, or meat.

In Praise of Being Peripheral

Without philosophy,
tragedy,
history,

a gray squirrel
looks
very busy.

Light as a soul
released
from a painting by Bosch,
its greens
and vermilions stripped off it.

He climbs a tree
that is equally ahistoric.

His heart works harder.

A Chair in Snow

A chair in snow
should be
like any other object whited
& rounded

and yet a chair in snow is always sad

more than a bed
more than a hat or house
a chair is shaped for just one thing

to hold
a soul its quick and few bendable
hours

perhaps a king

not to hold snow
not to hold flowers

LIKE THE SMALL HOLE BY THE PATH-SIDE SOMETHING LIVES IN

Like the small hole by the path-side something lives in,
in me are lives I do not know the names of,

nor the fates of,
nor the hungers of or what they eat.

They eat of me.
Of small and blemished apples in low fields of me
whose rocky streams and droughts I do not drink.

And in my streets—the narrow ones,
unlabeled on the self-map—
they follow stairs down music ears can't follow,

and in my tongue borrowed by darkness,
in hours uncounted by the self-clock,
they speak in restless syllables of other losses, other loves.

There too have been the hard extinctions,
missing birds once feasted on and feasting.

There too must be machines
like loud ideas with tungsten bits that grind the day.

A few escape. A mercy.

They leave behind
small holes that something unweighed by the self-scale lives in.

Wet Spring

The practical castle is cold.
All around it the world is a stream bed.

A few well-placed openings
under the windows
let rain weep back outward.

The rain is string
for wrapping a package no one knows
the inside of, they just keep trying to mail it.

Perhaps it is licorice. Perhaps it is kindness.

The package so large even wetness becomes an umbrella.

MANY-ROOFED BUILDING IN MOONLIGHT

I found myself
suddenly voluminous,
three-dimensioned,
a many-roofed building in moonlight.

Thought traversed
me as simply as moths might.
Feelings traversed me as fish.

I heard myself thinking,
It isn't the piano, it isn't the ears.

Then heard, too soon, the ordinary furnace,
the usual footsteps above me.

Washed my face again with hot water,
as I did when I was a child.

Anywhere You Look

in the corner of a high rain gutter
under the roof tiles
new grasses' delicate seed heads

what war, they say

ANATOMY AND MAKING

In Chinese painting, there are flowers with bones,
flowers that are boneless.

Also in trees, men, mountains, horses, and houses.

A calcium not subject
but angle
the brush is held by, minerals into.

Fox hairs are soft,
yet fox bones and fox teeth are in them.

Dragon veins, the space between mountains is called.

Lu Ch'ai wrote, "When painting a rock, paint all three of its faces."

I think of the two Greek masks, one laughing, one weeping,
and then of the third he would have found missing—
mask-face of wonder? of anger? of rigor?
a child's look before sleep?

Lu wrote,
"There is only one thing to be said here: rocks painted fully are living."
And then, of painting people,
"Hands slipped into sleeves are warm, no feeling of coldness."

I Cast My Hook,
I Decide to Make Peace

The bee does not speak to me.
The whale does not speak to me.
The horse is silent.

History does not speak to me.
Arachne is only a spider.

Nothing says "you" if I offer "I,"
"I" if I proffer "you."

I would go
to the Counter of Complaining—

there was one,
a hut of new pine wood
at the base of the Yellow Mountains in China,
the door was open, a woman sat in the chair—

but nothing says "counter,"
nothing says "yellow" or "mountain."

Erased dust of the chalkboard, barnacle,
less *sleep* than *bed*—
what can I do, faceless, with no one to kiss or shout at?

I cast my hook, my vote against it,
I decide to make peace.

I declare this intention but nothing answers.
And so I put peace in a warm place, towel-covered, to proof,
then into an oven. I wait.
Peace is patient and undemanding, it *surpasseth*.

And the bulldozers move
from the palace of breaking to the places of building.
And the students return to their classes.
Tuna swim freely.
The sky hoists the flag of the sky.

All this in the space of a half-page, a little ink,
a small bite of hubris
sweetened with raisins and honey.

I begin to consider what I will make of tomorrow's speechless.

A PERSON PROTESTS TO FATE

A person protests to fate:

"The things you have caused
me most to want
are those that furthest elude me."

Fate nods.
Fate is sympathetic.

To tie the shoes, button a shirt,
are triumphs
for only the very young,
the very old.

During the long middle:

conjugating a rivet
mastering tango
training the cat to stay off the table
preserving a single moment longer than this one
continuing to wake whatever has happened the day before

and the penmanships love practices inside the body.

Twelve Pebbles

A Hand Holds One Power

A hand holds one power,
whose exercise requires the hand be empty.

The Woman, The Tiger

The woman, the tiger, the door, the man, the choice.

Riddles are soulless.
In them, it is never raining.

Tri-Focal

the cat sleeping
paw prints of bear in the road-sand
a day moth confusedly walking the glass between them

I Know You Think I've Forgotten

but today
in rain

without coat without hat

Still Life

Loyalty of a book
to its place on the shelf
in a still life.

Like that,
the old loves continue.

A man I once asked a question of has died; his son sends a letter.

A thirsty mouse turns a river.
A stone turns a river.

Bodiless words turn us.

Human Measures

a woman in a distant language sings with great feeling
the composer's penciled-in instructions to sing with great feeling.

Immigration & Hunger

I misread the journalist's sentence:
"In this human drama, the police ate the supporting actors."

Humbling: An Assay

Have teeth.

For Fifteen Years

A woman says to her daughter,
for fifteen years,
"For the first time now,
I am feeling my age, for the first time."

A blessed life.
Each day's yesterday was joyous.
Each year completed was good.

A map open on one table, a guidebook on the other

"I am here.
I want to be nowhere but here,"
says the still hanging apricot,
growing rounder
like a page from Lewis Carroll.

Making & Passing

New new new new new
bluster the young birds in spring.
An old branch holds them.
Generation.
Strange word: both making and passing.

———•◆•———

I Wanted Only a Little

I wanted, I thought, only a little,
two teaspoons of silence—
one for sugar,
one for stirring the wetness.

No.
I wanted a Cairo of silence,
a Kyoto.
In every hanging garden
mosses and waters.

The directions of silence:
north, west, south, past, future.

It comes through any window
one inch open,
like rain driven sideways.

Grief shifts,
as a grazing horse does,
one leg to the other.

But a horse sleeping
sleeps with all legs locked.

A Common Cold

A common cold, we say—
common, though it has encircled the globe
    seven times now handed traveler to traveler
    though it has seen the Wild Goose Pagoda in Xi'an
    seen Piero della Francesca's *Madonna del Parto* in Monterchi
    seen the emptied synagogues of Krasnogruda
    seen the since-burned souk of Aleppo

A common cold, we say—
common, though it is infinite and surely immortal
    common because it will almost never kill us
    and because it is shared among any who agree to or do not agree to
    and because it is unaristocratic
        reducing to redness both profiled and front-viewed noses
        reducing to coughing the once-articulate larynx
        reducing to unhappy sleepless turning the pillows of down,
            of wool, of straw, of foam, of kapok

A common cold, we say—
common because it is cloudy and changing and dulling
    because there are summer colds, winter colds, fall colds,
        colds of the spring
    because these are always called colds, however they differ
        beginning sore-throated
        beginning sniffling
        beginning a little tired or under the weather
        beginning with one single innocuous untitled sneeze
    because it is bane of usually eight days' duration
        and two or three boxes of tissues at most

The common cold, we say—
and wonder, when did it join us

when did it saunter into the Darwinian corridors of the human
do manatees catch them do parrots I do not think so
and who named it first, first described it, Imhotep, Asclepius,
   Zhongjing
and did they wonder, is it happy sharing our lives
      as generously as inexhaustibly as it shares its own
      virus dividing and changing while Piero's girl gazes still
         downward
      five centuries still waiting still pondering still undivided

while in front of her someone hunts through her opening pockets for tissues
      for more than one reason at once

THIS MORNING, I WANTED FOUR LEGS

Nothing on two legs weighs much,
or can.
An elephant, a donkey, even a cookstove—
those legs, a person could stand on.
Two legs pitch you forward.
Two legs tire.
They look for another two legs to be with,
to move one set forward to music
while letting the other move back.
They want to carve into a tree trunk:
2gether 4ever.
Nothing on two legs can bark,
can whinny or chuff.
Tonight, though, everything's different.
Tonight I want wheels.

Once, I

Once, I
was seven Spanish bullocks in a high meadow,
sleepy and nameless.

As-ifness strange to myself, but complete.

Light on the neck-nape
of time
as two wings of one starling,

or lovers so happy
neither needs think of the other.

In Daylight, I Turned on the Lights

In daylight, I turned on the lights,
in darkness, I pulled closed the curtains.
And the god of More,
whom nothing surprises, softly agreed—
each day, year after year,
the dead were dead one day more completely.
In the places where morels were found,
I looked for morels.
In the houses where love was found,
I looked for love.
If she is vanished, what then was different?
If he is alive, what now is changed?
The pot offers the metal closest to fire for burning.
The water leaves.

How Rarely I Have Stopped
to Thank the Steady Effort

A person speaking
pauses, lets in
a little silence-portion with the words.
It is like an hour.
Any hour. This one.
Something happens, much does not.
Or as always, everything happens:
the standing walls keep
standing with their whole attention.
A noisy crow call lowers and lifts its branch,
the crow scent enters the leaves, enters the bark,
like stirred-in honey gone into the tea.
How rarely I have stopped to thank
the steady effort of the world to stay the world.
To thank the furnish of green
and abandon of yellow. The ancient Sumerians
called the beloved "Honey," as we do.
Said also, "Borrowed bread is not returned."
Like them, we pay love's tax to bees,
we go on arranging the old notes in different orders.
Desire inside A C A G G A T.
Forgiveness in G T A C T T.
In a world of space and time, arrangement matters.
An hour has no front or back,
except to those whose eyes face forward,
whose tears blur thought and stars.
Five genes, in a certain arrangement,
will spend this life unrooted, grazing.
It has to do with how the animal body comes into being,
the same whether ant or camel.
What then does such unfolded code understand,
if it finds in its mouth the word *important*—

the thing that can be carried, or the thing that cannot,
or the way they keep trading places,
grief and gladness, the comic, the glum, the dead, the living.
Last night, the big Sumerian moon
clambered into the house empty-handed
and left empty-handed,
not thief, not lover, not tortoise, just looking around,
shuffling its soft, blind slippers over the floor.
This felt, to me, important, and so I looked back with both hands
open, palms unblinking.
What caused the fire, we ask, meaning, *lightning, wiring, matches.*
How precisely and unbidden
oxygen slips itself into, between those thick words.

As a Hammer Speaks to a Nail

When all else fails,
fail boldly,
fail with conviction,
as a hammer speaks to a nail,
or a lamp left on in daylight.

Say *one*.
If *two* does not follow,
say *three*, if that fails, say *life*,
say *future*.

Lacking *future*,
try *bucket*,
lacking *iron*, try *shadow*.

If *shadow* too fails,
if your voice falls and falls and keeps falling,
meets only air and silence,

say *one* again,
but say it with greater conviction,

as a nail speaks to a picture,
as a hammer left on in daylight.

I Sat in the Sun

I moved my chair into sun
I sat in the sun
the way hunger is moved when called fasting.

OF AMPLITUDE
THERE IS NO SCRAPING BOTTOM

In certain styles of Chinese painting,
three diagonal brushstrokes balance a mountain.
Like that, the word for happiness
keeps inside it the word for chance. For haplessness, also.
You wanted to be ignorant, unknowing, thunderstruck, gobsmacked.
Wanted to be brought to your knees
by the scent of mushrooms you couldn't know whether to pick.
When the violent, brilliant goshawk,
excessive and unforgiving, drove you from her nesting,
she battered your head with its own blunt weight of animal being.
The big, deaf bear in both lanes of the dark
was a grandmother's fake pearl necklace suddenly real.
You ate the stories of others
because your own were already inside you and you were still hungry.
You wanted to sleep in a house you could walk the outside of,
windowed and simple, and find on it one day a door—
green-peeling, padlocked—you'd never guessed at.
You found the house, you entered, ate there, slept.
But however you rummaged and plundered the inside,
that door, that blind-hinged door, kept opening elsewhere.

THE ONE NOT CHOSEN

Third sister,
aunt one forgets to send a card to.

Boy on a bench, second smallest,
not quick, not precise, not cunning.

Culled chick, branch-bruised peach,
chair wobbly, unused, set in a corner.

For some, almost good, almost lucky
not to be chosen,
though equally accidental—
the thirty-year-buried land mine
chooses the leg of another.
(How the mouth struggles
to say it: lucky, good.)

Most are not chosen, most mostly watch.
So it must be.
The watched
(not escaping pride, not truly minding)
bemoan their responsibilities,
so many anxieties, demands, complications.

And still: any rabbit the center
of its own rabbit world,
its universe axis a nest of tamped-down grasses.

It looks out its ground-level eyes,
is warm, is curious, hungry,
its heart beats faster or slower
with its own rabbit fate.

A rabbit's soul cannot help
but choose its own ears, its own paws,
its own startlement, sleepiness, longings,
it has a rabbit allegiance,

and the pink nose, which
could have been drawn in charcoal
by Dürer's sister, but wasn't,
takes in its own warmth and fur-scent,
glints pinkly,
pinkly alters the distant star's light
in its own cuniculan corner
among vast and unanswerable worlds,
without even knowing it does so.

Snow in April

"There, there," the awkward uncle
comforts
the crying infant.

"There, there," he repeats,
agreeing:
Here, here is the only possible problem.

Soon now, *there* and *here*
will both move along,
a lullaby about snow falling in a snowy pasture.

February 29

An extra day—

Like the painting's fifth cow,
who looks out directly,
straight toward you,
from inside her black and white spots.

An extra day—

Accidental, surely:
the made calendar stumbling over the real
as a drunk trips over a threshold
too low to see.

An extra day—

With a second cup of black coffee.
A friendly but businesslike phone call.
A mailed-back package.
Some extra work, but not too much—
just one day's worth, exactly.

An extra day—

Not unlike the space
between a door and its frame
when one room is lit and another is not,
and one changes into the other
as a woman exchanges a scarf.

An extra day—

Extraordinarily like any other.
And still
there is some generosity to it,
like a letter re-readable after its writer has died.

THREE MORNINGS

In Istanbul, my ears
three mornings heard the early call to prayer.
At fuller light, heard birds then,
waterbirds and tree birds, birds of migration.
Like three knowledges,
I heard them: incomprehension,
sweetened distance, longing.
When the body dies, where will they go,
those migrant birds and prayer calls,
as heat from sheets when taken from a dryer?
With voices of the ones I loved,
great loves and small loves, train wheels,
crickets, clock-ticks, thunder—where will they,
when in fragrant, tumbled heat they also leave?

Away from Home,
I Thought of the Exiled Poets

Away from home,
I read the exiled poets—
Ovid, Brecht.

Then set my books that night
near the foot of the bed.

All night pretended they were the cat.

Not once
did I wake her.

All Souls

In Italy, on the day of the dead,
they ring bells,
from every church and village in every direction.
At the usual times, the regular bells of the hour—
eleven strokes, twelve. Oar strokes
laid over and into the bottomless water and air.
But the others? Tuneless, keyless,
rhythm of wings at the door of the hive
when the entrance is suddenly shuttered
and the bees, returned heavy, see
that the world of flowering and pollen is over.
There can be no instruction
to make this. Undimensioned
the tongues of the bells,
the ropes of the bells, their big iron bodies unholy.
Barred from form, barred from bars,
from relation. The beauty—unspeakable—
was beauty. I drank it and thirsted,
I stopped. I ran. Wanted closer in every direction.
Each bell stroke released without memory
or judgment, unviolent, untender. Uncaring.
And yet: existent. Something trembling.
I—who have not known bombardment—
have never heard so naked a claim
of the dead on the living, to know them.

In Space

In space
(the experiment
suggested by two fifth graders),
a Canadian astronaut
wrings water out of a towel.

It stays by the towel,
horizontal
transparent isinglass,
a hyaline column.

Then begins to cover his hands,
his wrists,
stays on them
until he passes it to another towel.

On earth
some who watch this
recognize the wrung, irrational soul.

How it does not leave
but stays close,
outside the cleaning twist-fate but close—

fear   desire   anger
joy   irritation
mourning

wet stuff
that is shining, that cannot go from us,
having nowhere other to fall.

SOUVENIR

I would like
to take something with me

but even one chair
is too awkward
too heavy

peeling paint
falls off in a suitcase
hinge sounds betray a theft
cheeses won't keep

the clothespin
without its surroundings
would be mediocre

the big thunder rolled elsewhere

the umbrella is for sale
but in a desert what you want is a soaking

the do not disturb sign is tattered

I have many times taken
some café's small packets of sugar
so that in Turkey
I might sweeten my coffee with China,
and in Italy remember a Lithuanian pastry

but where is the coffee

hands left and right useless

knees clattery
heart finally calm
as some hero at the end of a movie
squinting silently into the sun

you can't hold an umbrella there anyhow
and what would he hang from the clothespin

The Must-Mice

Any hour is grain bin,
fragrant, many.

Soon the must-mice come.

Each takes
its one-mouse mouthful,
and is filled.

The bin empties
to its wooden sides and floor.

Hunger that
comes and goes
turns time into memory.

Mouthful
by mouse-sized mouthful,

houseful
by vanishing houseful.

THE CONVERSATIONS I REMEMBER MOST

The way a sweet cake wants
a little salt in it,
or blackness a little gray nearby to be seen,
or a pot unused stays good for boiling water,

the conversations I remember most
are the ones that were interrupted.

Wait, you say, running after them,
I forgot to ask—

Night rain, they answer.
Silver on the fire-thorn's red berries.

Two Linen Handkerchiefs

How can you have been dead twelve years
and these still

Works & Loves

1.

Rain fell as a glass
breaks,
something suddenly everywhere at the same time.

2.

To live like a painting
looked into from more than one angle at once—

eye to eye with the doorway
down at the hair
up at your own dusty feet.

3.

"This is your house,"
said my bird heart to my heart of the cricket,
and I entered.

4.

The happy see only happiness,
the living see only life,
the young see only the young.

As lovers believe
they wake always beside one also in love.

5.

However often I turned its pages,
I kept ending up
as the same two sentences of the book:

The being of some is: to be. Of others: to be without.

Then I fell back asleep, in Swedish.

6.

A sheep grazing is unimpressed by the mountain
but not by its flies.

7.

The grief
of what hasn't yet happened—

a door closed from inside

the weight of the grass
dividing
an ant's five-legged contemplations
walking through it.

8.

What is the towel, what is the water,
changes,
though of we three,
only the towel can be held upside down in the sun.

9.

"I was once."
Said not in self-pity or praise.
This dignity we allow barn owl,
ego, oyster.

Perspective Without Any Point in Which It Might Vanish

The way the green or blue or yellow in a painting
is simply green and yellow and blue,
and *tree* is, *boat* is, *sky* is
in them also—

There are worlds
in which nothing is adjective, everything noun.

This among them.

Even today—this falling day—
it might be so.
Footstep, footstep, footstep intimate on it.

RUNNER

It is hard to unlatch a day
from noun and story.

Breath pours
like water
from a small bowl into a large.

One says,
Quicker.

Another,
Listen, runner—
underwater things are fragrant to a fish.

THE BEAUTIFUL AUSTERE ROOM

This beautiful austere room—

(room in which you are dying,
room in which $a - a$
will still $= a$,
world – world = world)

I bring it flowers.

They hold themselves
up from the water with effort,
an aging woman
walking up Eighty-Sixth Street,
slowly,
in painful pink shoes and pink gloves.

Not One Moment of This
a Subtraction

all day the daylight coming over the sill
like a wagon
drawn by invisible big-hooved horses working hard

soon now your breathing will climb inside it, go with it away

all your mountains and rivers
your cities and memories
doing their silent handsprings inside it

I Profess the Uncertain

I profess the uncertain
with gratitude

a man with large hands
and large feet
first looks at a pencil
then brings it close to his ear

he listens

the day lives briefly
unscented

shaken with worn-heel glimpses

becomes a shambling palace
with walking fishes
a yellow-roofed kindness

the almost untenable premise
that between counting one and two
nothing is lost

ZERO PLUS ANYTHING IS A WORLD

Four less one is three.

Three less two is one.

One less three
is what, is who,
remains.

The first cell that learned to divide
learned to subtract.

Recipe:
add salt to hunger.

Recipe:
add time to trees.

Zero plus anything
is a world.

This one
and no other,
unhidden,
by each breath changed.

Recipe:
add death to life.

Recipe:
love without swerve what this will bring.

Sister, father, mother, husband, daughter.

Like a cello
forgiving one note as it goes,
then another.

ENTANGLEMENT

A librarian in Calcutta and an entomologist in Prague
sign their moon-faced illicit emails,
"ton entanglée."

No one can explain it.
The strange charm between border collie and sheep,
leaf and wind, the two distant electrons.

There is, too, the matter of a horse race.
Each person shouts for his own horse louder,
confident in the rising din
past whip, past mud,
the horse will hear his own name in his own quickened ear.

Desire is different:
desire is the moment before the race is run.

Has an electron never refused
the invitation to change direction,
sent in no knowable envelope, with no knowable ring?

A story told often: after the lecture, the widow
insisting the universe rests on the back of a turtle.
And what, the physicist
asks, does the turtle rest on?

Very clever, young man, she replies, very clever,
but it's turtles all the way down.

And so a woman in Beijing buys for her love,
who practices turtle geometry in Boston, a metal trinket
from a night-market street stall.

On the back of a turtle, at rest on its shell,
a turtle.
Inside that green-painted shell, another, still smaller.

This continues for many turtles,
until finally, too small to see
or to lift up by its curious, preacherly head,
a single un-green electron
waits the width of a world for some weightless message
sent into the din of existence for it alone.

Murmur of all that is claspable, clabberable, clamberable,
against all that is not:

You are there. I am here. I remember.

LIKE TWO NEGATIVE NUMBERS
MULTIPLIED BY RAIN

Lie down, you are horizontal.
Stand up, you are not.

I wanted my fate to be human.

Like a perfume
that does not choose the direction it travels,
that cannot be straight or crooked, kept out or kept.

Yes, No, Or
—a day, a life, slips through them,
taking off the third skin,
taking off the fourth.

The logic of shoes becomes at last simple,
an animal question, scuffing.

Old shoes, old roads—
the questions keep being new ones.
Like two negative numbers multiplied by rain
into oranges and olives.

Acknowledgments

The author is grateful to Civitella Ranieri, the MacDowell Colony, and Yaddo, under whose generous hospitality many of these poems were written. Also to the journals in which some of these poems first appeared, sometimes in different versions.

The American Poetry Review: "Cellophane: An Assay," "Florists' Roses," "I Cast My Hook, I Decide to Make Peace," "I Wake Early," "Two Linen Handkerchiefs"

ARTS: "Perspective Without Any Point in Which It Might Vanish"

The Atlantic: "Perspective: An Assay"

The Cortland Review: "Honey," "I Profess the Uncertain"

Discover: "Entanglement"

Five Points: "A Well Runs Out of Thirst," "In Praise of Being Peripheral," "My Sandwich" (as "A Cottage Cheese Sandwich") (U.S., reprint), "Ordinary Rain. Every Leaf Is Wet.," "Still Life" (as "Old Love")

Great River Review: "A Hand Holds One Power," "A man I once asked a question of has died; his son sends a letter," "A map open on one table, a guidebook on the other," "Anywhere You Look," "The Beautiful Austere Room," "Human Measures," "Humbling: An Assay," "I Know You Think I've Forgotten," "Immigration & Hunger," "Making & Passing," "Still Life," "Tri-focal"

Harper's: "A Cottony Fate" (reprint)

The Harvard Divinity School Bulletin: "Runner," "Three Mornings"

The Irish Times (Ireland): "February 29"

The Kenyon Review: "Mosquito" (as "My Pronoun"), "Of Amplitude There Is No Scraping Bottom"

Mission at Tenth: "Quartz Clock"

The New Republic: "Anatomy and Making"

The New Yorker: "In Daylight, I Turned on the Lights," "I Wanted Only a Little," "My Corkboard," "My Life Was the Size of My Life," "My Proteins," "This Morning, I Wanted Four Legs"

The New York Times: "How Rarely I Have Stopped to Thank the Steady Effort"

Orion: "Not One Moment of This a Subtraction"

The Paris Review: "A Cottony Fate"

Ploughshares: "Hamper," "In a Kitchen Where Mushrooms Were Washed," "Mop Without Stick"

Plume: "As a Hammer Speaks to a Nail," "The Conversations I Remember Most," "In a Room with Many Windows," "Zero Plus Anything Is a World" (U.S., reprint)

Poetry: "A Chair in Snow," "Fado," "I Sat in the Sun," "Like the Small Hole by the Path-Side Something Lives In," "Like Two Negative Numbers Multiplied by Rain," "My Eyes" (as "An Hour Is Not a House"), "My Species," "My Weather," "Once, I," "The Problem," "Souvenir," "Things Keep Sorting Themselves," "Works & Loves"

Poetry Daily (poems.com): "A Common Cold" (reprint)

Poetry London (UK): "In My Wallet I Carry a Card," "My Sandwich" (as "A Cottage Cheese Sandwich"), "Zero Plus Anything Is A World"

Poets.org Poem-A-Day: "Many-Roofed Building in Moonlight," "My Skeleton," "A Person Protests to Fate"

Spillway: "Snow in April"

Spiritus: "In Space"

The Stony Thursday Book (Ireland): "All Souls," "How Rarely I Have Stopped to Thank the Steady Effort," "In Space" (all reprints)

The Telegraph (Calcutta, India): "In Daylight, I Turned on the Lights" (reprint)

The Threepenny Review: "A Common Cold"

Tin House: "The One Not Chosen"

West Marin Review: "Many-Roofed Building in Moonlight" (reprint)

Certain poems first appeared in the following anthologies:

The Alhambra Poetry Calendar: "In Daylight, I Turned on the Lights"; *The Best American Poetry 2015:* "A Common Cold," *The Best American Poetry 2012:* "In a Kitchen Where Mushrooms Were Washed"; *The Best Spiritual Writing 2012:* "In Daylight, I Turned on the Lights"; *The Bloomsbury Anthology of Contemporary Jewish American Poetry:* "In a Kitchen Where Mushrooms Were Washed"; *The Plume Anthology 2012:* "All Souls," "Immigration & Hunger," "The Woman, The Tiger"; *The Plume Anthology 2014:* "A Photograph of a Face Half Lit, Half in Darkness"; *The Pushcart Prize Anthology XXXVII:* "In a Kitchen Where Mushrooms Were Washed"

A number of the poems in this collection also appeared in a limited-edition letterpress chapbook, *Minus/My-ness*, published by Missing Links Press, and in letterpress broadsides by printer Jerry Reddan, in his Tangram series.

A Note About the Author

Jane Hirshfield is the author of eight books of poetry, including *The Beauty; Come, Thief; After;* and *Given Sugar, Given Salt.* She has edited and co-translated four books presenting the work of poets from the past and is the author of two major collections of essays, *Nine Gates: Entering the Mind of Poetry* and *Ten Windows: How Great Poems Transform the World.* Her books have been finalists for the National Book Critics Circle Award and England's T. S. Eliot Prize; they have been named best books of the year by *The Washington Post, San Francisco Chronicle,* Amazon, and England's *Financial Times;* and they have won the California Book Award, the Poetry Center Book Award, and the Donald Hall–Jane Kenyon Prize in American Poetry. Hirshfield has received fellowships from the Guggenheim and Rockefeller foundations, the National Endowment for the Arts, and the Academy of American Poets. Her poems have appeared in *The New Yorker, The Atlantic, The Times Literary Supplement, The Washington Post, The New York Times, Harper's, Poetry, Orion, Discover, The American Poetry Review, McSweeney's, The Pushcart Prize* anthology, and seven editions of *The Best American Poetry.* A resident of Northern California since 1974, she presents her poems in universities, literary centers, and festivals throughout the United States and abroad. She is a current chancellor of the Academy of American Poets.

A NOTE ON THE TYPE

Pierre Simon Fournier *le jeune* (1712–1768), who designed the type used in this book, was both an originator and a collector of types. His services to the art of printing were his design of letters, his creation of ornaments and initials, and his standardization of type sizes. His types are old style in character and sharply cut. In 1764 and 1766 he published his *Manuel typographique*, a treatise on the history of French types and printing, on typefounding in all its details, and on what many consider his most important contribution to typography—the measurement of type by the point system.

Composed by Scribe,
Philadelphia, Pennsylvania

Printed and bound by Berryville Graphics,
Berryville, Virginia

Designed by Betty Lew